GAP YEAR

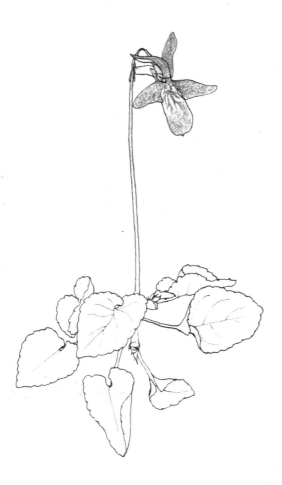

Traveller's Joy, like Virgin's Bower of North America, is a *Clematis* which replaces the big showy flowers of its garden relative with a multitude of smaller flowers. The flowers are a greenish-cream color and the petals are thick and fuzzy.

Ragged Robin
(*Lychnis flos-cuculi*)
West Highland Way, Scotland

Traveller's Joy.
(*Clematis vitalba*)
Whitbarrow, England

↑ 3x, c.s.

Birdsfoot Tre
(*Lotus cornicu*

← Common Spotted Orchid
(*Dactylorhiza fuschsii*)

Alnmouth,
England

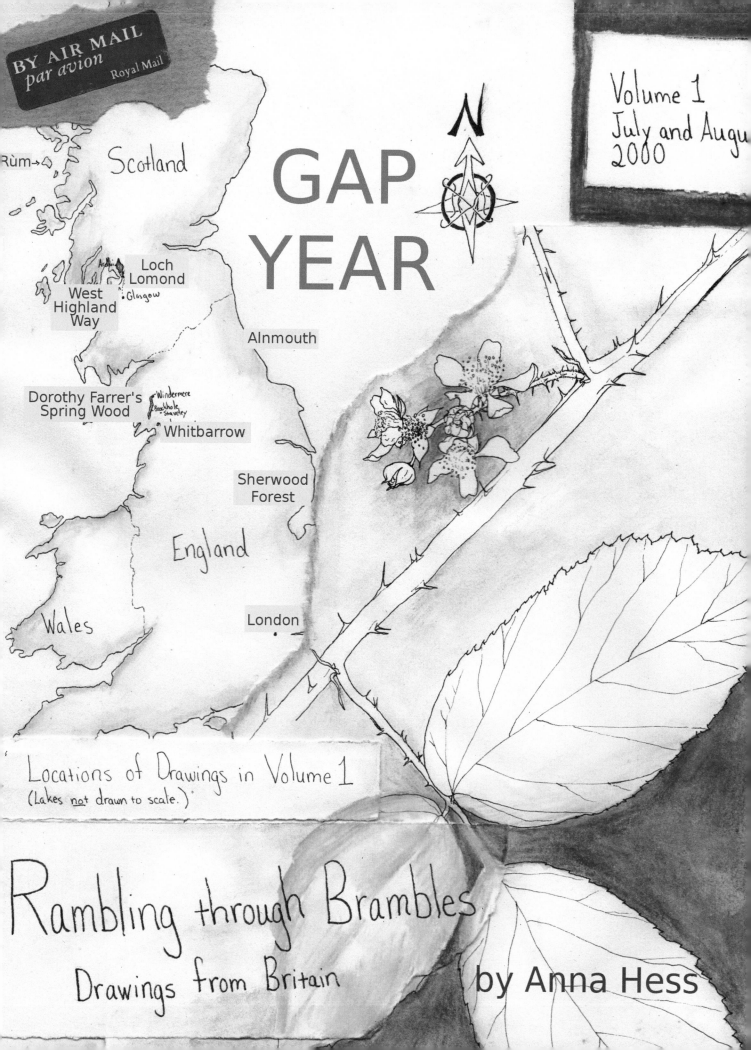

BY AIR MAIL
par avion Royal Mail

Scotland

Rùm→

Arran
Loch
Lomond
West
Highland
Way
Glasgow

Alnmouth

Dorothy Farrer's
Spring Wood
Windermere
Brockhole
Staveley
Whitbarrow

Sherwood
Forest

England

Wales

London

GAP
YEAR

N

Volume 1
July and Augu
2000

Locations of Drawings in Volume 1
(Lakes *not* drawn to scale.)

Rambling through Brambles

Drawings from Britain   by Anna Hess

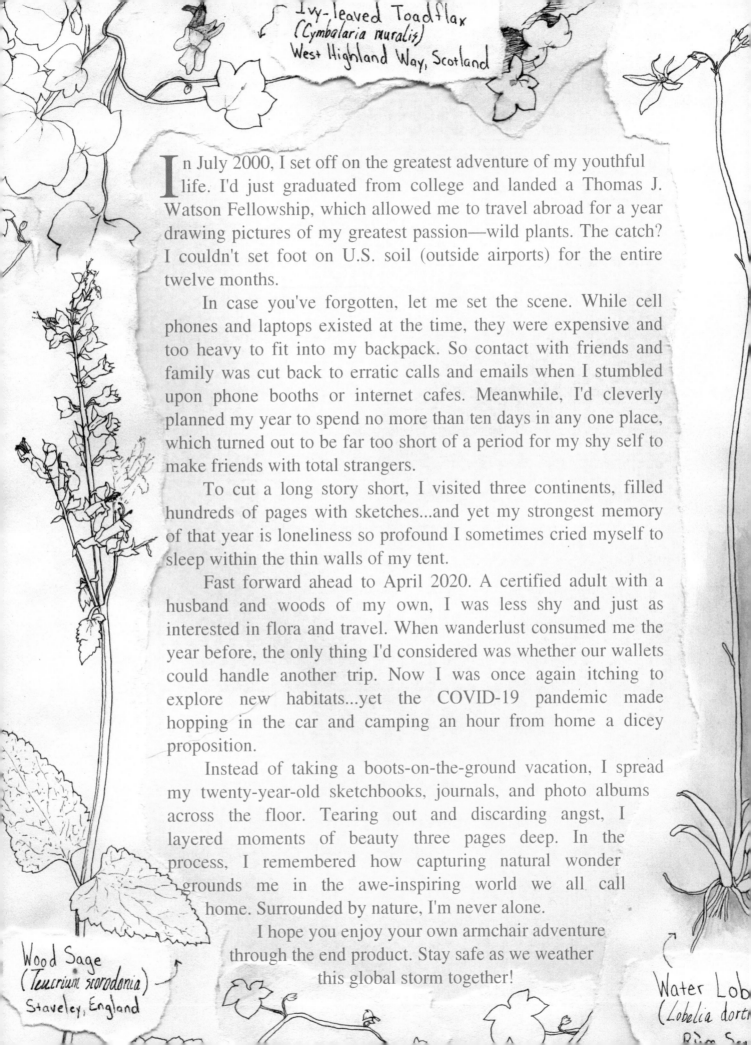

Ivy-leaved Toadflax
(Cymbalaria muralis)
West Highland Way, Scotland

In July 2000, I set off on the greatest adventure of my youthful life. I'd just graduated from college and landed a Thomas J. Watson Fellowship, which allowed me to travel abroad for a year drawing pictures of my greatest passion—wild plants. The catch? I couldn't set foot on U.S. soil (outside airports) for the entire twelve months.

In case you've forgotten, let me set the scene. While cell phones and laptops existed at the time, they were expensive and too heavy to fit into my backpack. So contact with friends and family was cut back to erratic calls and emails when I stumbled upon phone booths or internet cafes. Meanwhile, I'd cleverly planned my year to spend no more than ten days in any one place, which turned out to be far too short of a period for my shy self to make friends with total strangers.

To cut a long story short, I visited three continents, filled hundreds of pages with sketches...and yet my strongest memory of that year is loneliness so profound I sometimes cried myself to sleep within the thin walls of my tent.

Fast forward ahead to April 2020. A certified adult with a husband and woods of my own, I was less shy and just as interested in flora and travel. When wanderlust consumed me the year before, the only thing I'd considered was whether our wallets could handle another trip. Now I was once again itching to explore new habitats...yet the COVID-19 pandemic made hopping in the car and camping an hour from home a dicey proposition.

Instead of taking a boots-on-the-ground vacation, I spread my twenty-year-old sketchbooks, journals, and photo albums across the floor. Tearing out and discarding angst, I layered moments of beauty three pages deep. In the process, I remembered how capturing natural wonder grounds me in the awe-inspiring world we all call home. Surrounded by nature, I'm never alone.

I hope you enjoy your own armchair adventure through the end product. Stay safe as we weather this global storm together!

Wood Sage
(Teucrium scorodonia)
Staveley, England

Water Lob
(Lobelia dort
Riv S

Rosebay Willowherb
Chamerion angustifolium

From the "Automatic Outlaw" machine in the visitor center

Leaves have 1 pair of leaflets and a terminal tendril.

7-4-00
Kew Gardens, London
12:30 PM
overcast & breezy
67.2°F

...naled.

Meadow Vetchling
(Lathyrus pratensis)

Scotland's thistle. The coin's edge reads "Nemo me impure lacessit."
"No one provokes me with impunity."

Wales' leek. The coin's edge reads "Pleidol wyf i'm cwlad."
"True am I to my country."

England's oak. The coin's edge reads "Decus et tutamen."
"An ornament and a safeguard."

Queen
on
back →

My favorite British pound coins - the ones with plants on them.

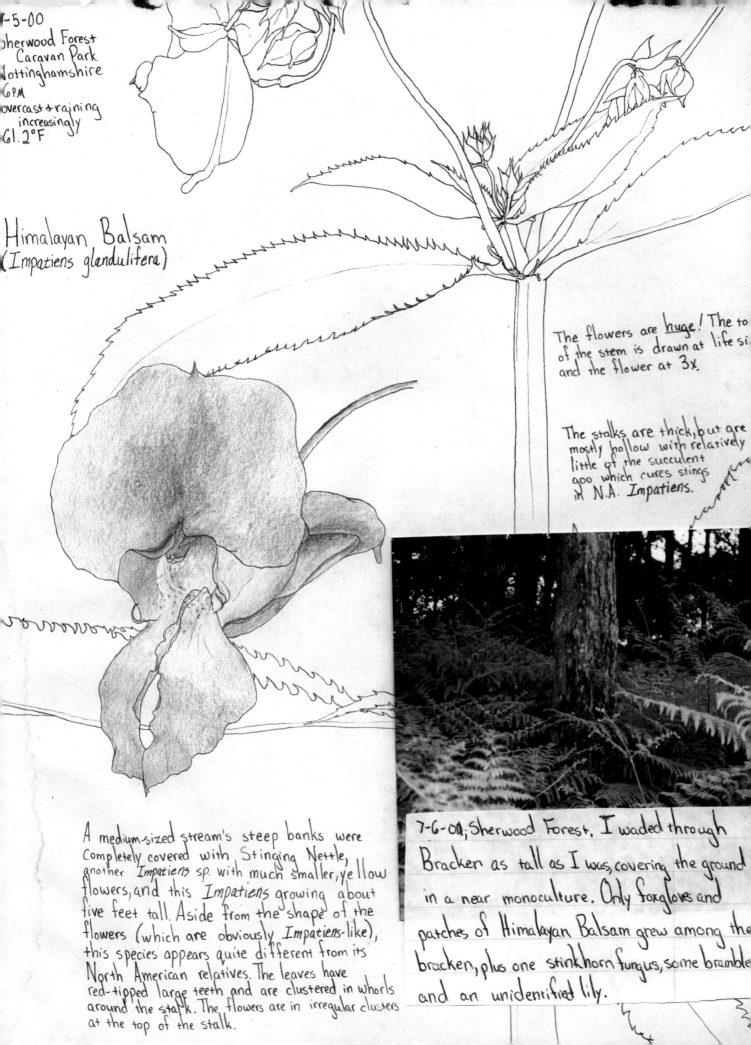

7-5-00
Sherwood Forest
    Caravan Park
Nottinghamshire
6 PM
overcast + raining
    increasing
61.2°F

Himalayan Balsam
(Impatiens glandulifera)

The flowers are <u>huge</u>! The top
of the stem is drawn at life si
and the flower at 3x.

The stalks are thick, but are
mostly hollow with relatively
little of the succulent
goo which cures stings
in N.A. *Impatiens*.

A medium-sized stream's steep banks were
completely covered with Stinging Nettle,
another *Impatiens* sp. with much smaller, yellow
flowers, and this *Impatiens* growing about
five feet tall. Aside from the shape of the
flowers (which are obviously *Impatiens*-like),
this species appears quite different from its
North American relatives. The leaves have
red-tipped large teeth and are clustered in whorls
around the stalk. The flowers are in irregular clusters
at the top of the stalk.

7-6-00; Sherwood Forest. I waded through
Bracken as tall as I was, covering the ground
in a near monoculture. Only foxgloves and
patches of Himalayan Balsam grew among the
bracken, plus one stinkhorn fungus, some bramble
and an unidentified lily.

Gear for a year

In addition to all this stuff, once I got out in the woods I had every extra nook and cranny of the Mammoth full of food.

7-7-00; Stealth camping in Alnmouth rather than risking Glasgow after d[...]

Binoculars.

Light t-shirt.

My huge, high tech watch tells the air temperature and time of sunset as well as more ordinary features.

Fanny pack- containing various papers, toothbrush, toothpaste, hairbrush, midge net, small budget notebook, coins, pens, pocketkni[...] fingernail scissors, sewing kit, and toilet paper.

The Mammoth, my backpack.

[W]ater is carried in [a] plastic water [b]ottle which fits [p]erfectly into a metal cup, and in a pouch inside the Mammoth with a hose so I can drink while walking.

Pockets are filled with a little notebook to jot down bird sightings, a wallet, a scrunchy, and various walnuts, rocks, and shells collected along the way.

Water hose.

Light pants with zip-off legs.

Water bottle.

Metal cup.

Heavy duty hiking boot[s] Underneath are two pairs of socks- a liner pair and a heavier pair

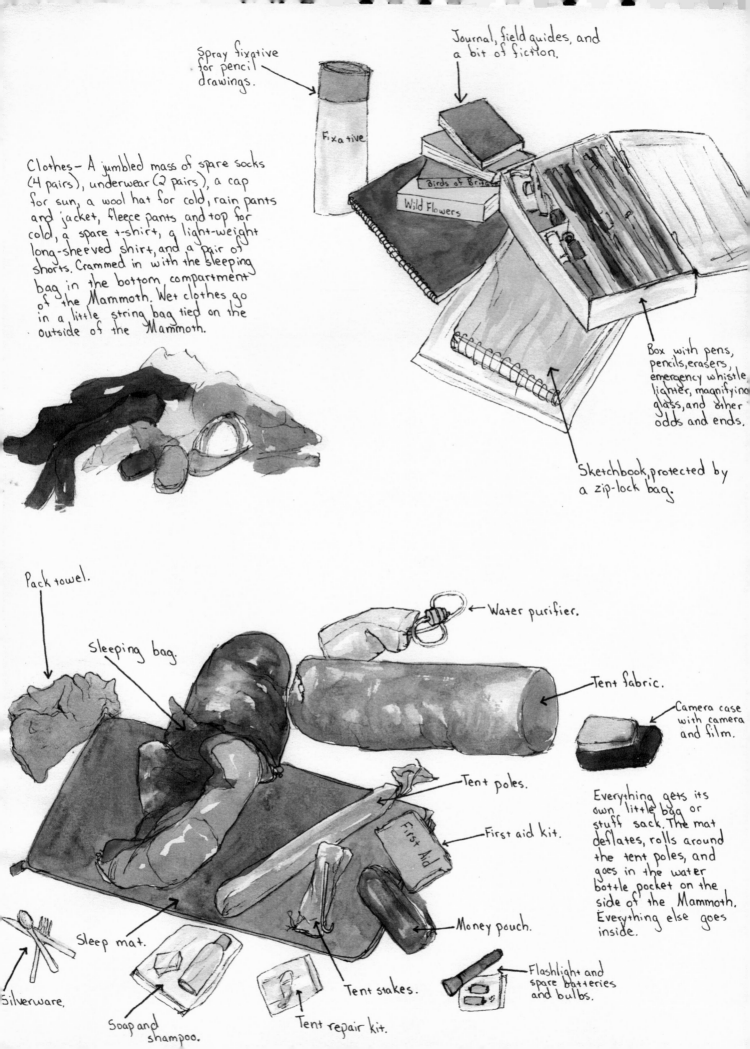

Spray fixative for pencil drawings.

Fixative

Journal, field guides, and a bit of fiction.

Birds of Brit...
Wild Flowers

Clothes— A jumbled mass of spare socks (4 pairs), underwear (2 pairs), a cap for sun, a wool hat for cold, rain pants and jacket, fleece pants and top for cold, a spare t-shirt, a light-weight long-sleeved shirt, and a pair of shorts. Crammed in with the sleeping bag in the bottom compartment of the Mammoth. Wet clothes go in a little string bag tied on the outside of the Mammoth.

Box with pens, pencils, erasers, emergency whistle, lighter, magnifying glass, and other odds and ends.

Sketchbook, protected by a zip-lock bag.

Pack towel.

Sleeping bag.

Water purifier.

Tent fabric.

Camera case with camera and film.

Tent poles.

First Aid

First aid kit.

Everything gets its own little bag or stuff sack. The mat deflates, rolls around the tent poles, and goes in the water bottle pocket on the side of the Mammoth. Everything else goes inside.

Money pouch.

Sleep mat.

Silverware.

Soap and shampoo.

Tent repair kit.

Tent stakes.

Flashlight and spare batteries and bulbs.

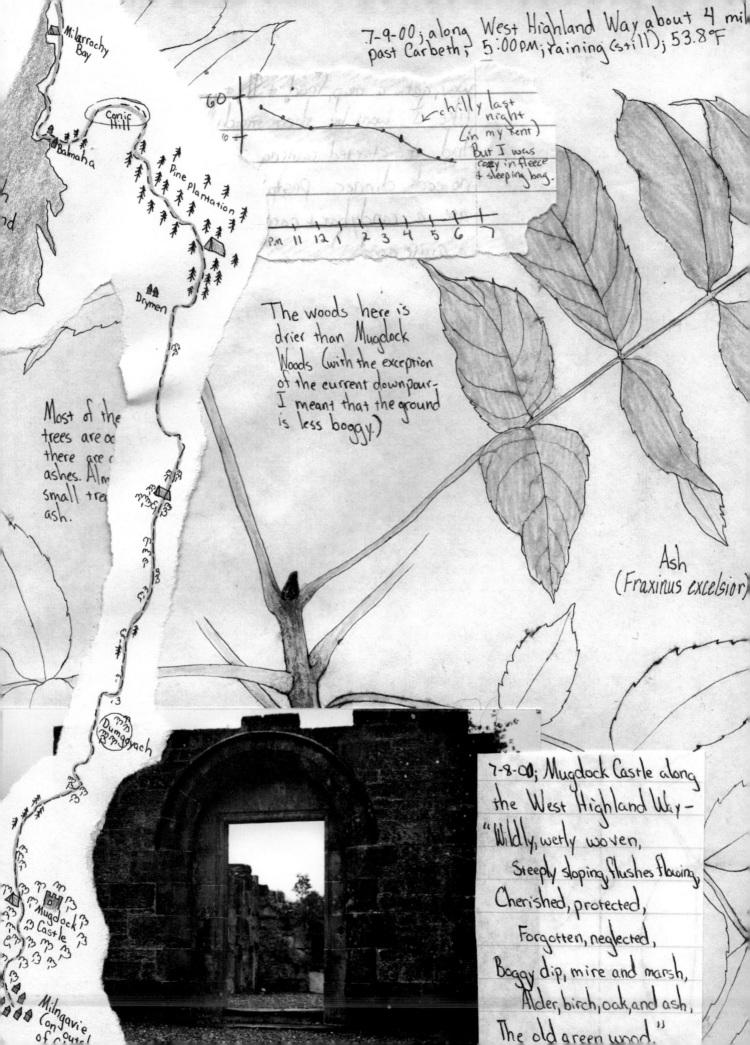

7-9-00; along West Highland Way about 4 mi[les]
past Carbeth; 5:00 PM; raining (still); 53.8°F

← chilly last night
(in my tent)
But I was cozy in fleece & sleeping bag.

60

PM 11 12 1 2 3 4 5 6 7

Milarrochy Bay

Conic Hill

Balmaha

Pine Plantation

Drymen

Most of the trees are oo[ak?]
there are [a?]
ashes. Alm[ost]
small tre[es]
ash.

The woods here is drier than Mugdock Woods (with the exception of the current downpour — I meant that the ground is less boggy.)

Dumgoyach

Ash
(Fraxinus excelsior)

Mugdock Castle

Milngavie
Con[way?]
out[side?]
of G[lasgow?]

7-8-00; Mugdock Castle along the West Highland Way —
"Wildly, wetly woven,
Steeply sloping, flushes flowing
Cherished, protected,
Forgotten, neglected,
Boggy dip, mire and marsh,
Alder, birch, oak, and ash,
The old green wood."

Unlike most cinquefoils, this species has only 4' (rather than 5) petals.

Tormentil
(*Potentilla erecta*)

Bog Cotton
or
Common Cotton-gr
(*Eriophorum angustifoliu*

← 1.75x

It's so strange to see treeless hills like this one. I'm up near the top and the groundcover is grasses and rushes and low bushes no more than a foot tall. Yellow Tormentil flowers dot the ground. And then there are these seed heads which look like white flowers against the grass.

Up close, I can see that they are really covered with tufts of white hairs. Each little tuft is attached to a seed and, eventually, the tuft comes loose and the seed is carried away on the wind.

7-11-00
West Highland Way, near the top of Conic Hill
partly cloudy, sunny, + windy
2:00 PM
65°F

Heath Speedwell
(*Veronica officinalis*)

← The f
the s
their

11-00: View from Conic Hill, showing a bit of Loch Lomond.

The paired leaves are on runner
which form a mat on the ground

Dear everybody,
 Well, my plans have changed yet again. After the first 20 miles of the West Highland Way, I found a campground on the shore of Loch Lomond & just stayed here for 4 days. I feel a little bad about giving up on the trail, but it just didn't work with my project. Too many sheep pastures and conifer plantations (the latter having nearly no life in it.) I also wasn't getting a good grasp on habitats since I was constantly moving on. Actually, the only reason I feel bad about verging from the Way is because of a stubbornness not to give up.
 So now I've been _____

By air mail
Par avion

23 JULY 2000 ... BRITAIN

Poct 034 Air out 45p

Common Sedge
(Carex nigra)

On the mossy clump at the base of the oak, the honeysuckle exists, as only a few vines. However, elsewhere in the woods, or out in the open, Honeysuckle is currently in bloom. The flowers, like the rest of the plant, are very similar to Japanese Honeysuck new flowers are white, while older flowe turn a yellow-orange. But unlike Japanese Honeysuckle, these flowers are tinged in red on the outside.

← 1.25x

1.25x ↓

Honeysuckle
(Lonicera periclymenum)

grasp of habitats, and so forth... so we've been beside Loch
Lomond ever since. The south part is like lakes at home
but the north part is truly a glacier-lake. It sits in
middle of mountains, where glaciers hollowed...

loch ↓

Watching a parent wagtail feeding its young.

Grateful that they're catching the clouds of biting midges. I ate breakfast on a swing in desperation...

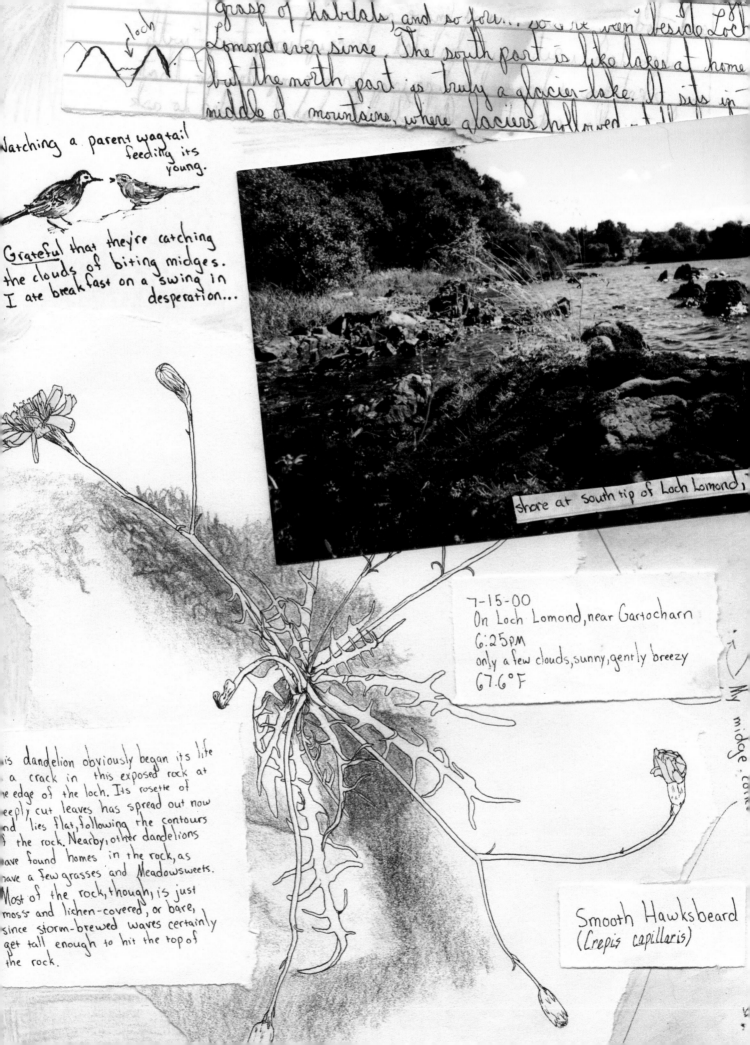

shore at South tip of Loch Lomond,

7-15-00
On Loch Lomond, near Gartocharn
6:25PM
only a few clouds, sunny, gently breezy
67.6°F

My midge coll...

is dandelion obviously began its life a crack in this exposed rock at e edge of the loch. Its rosette of eply cut leaves has spread out now nd lies flat, following the contours f the rock. Nearby, other dandelions ave found homes in the rock, as nave a few grasses and Meadowsweets. Most of the rock, though, is just moss and lichen-covered, or bare, since storm-brewed waves certainly get tall enough to hit the top of the rock.

Smooth Hawksbeard
(Crepis capillaris)

Deer here aren't quiet.
They bark like dogs!

7-14-00
Inchcailloch-island in
Loch Lomond, near Balmaha
1PM
partly cloudy+breezy
58.2°F

Ramsons
(Allium ursinum)

A colony of Ramsons is growing
in and beside a little ditch in a
relatively open area. At first glance,
seeing only the leaves, I thought it
might be some kind of dock. However,
the three-parted fruit placed it in
the Lily family. Then I noticed
the distinct, garlicky smell. Another
giveaway was the triangular flower
stalk.

West Highland Way

Milarrochy Bay

Balmaha

Loch Lomond

Inc

Gartocharn

The big difference is the public rights of way which let me walk
nearly anywhere. Fences either have steps to let you climb over, or little
gates which a person can go through, but not a sheep.

...Phew, my backpack fir throu
yet another one.

person
fence
from above

From side.

← sheep don't need barbed wire, jus
plain wire, apparently.

↳ steps to go over

I'm thinking this might be a stile (as in old lady who cou
...go over the stile.) Maybe... king great. The only Barmah

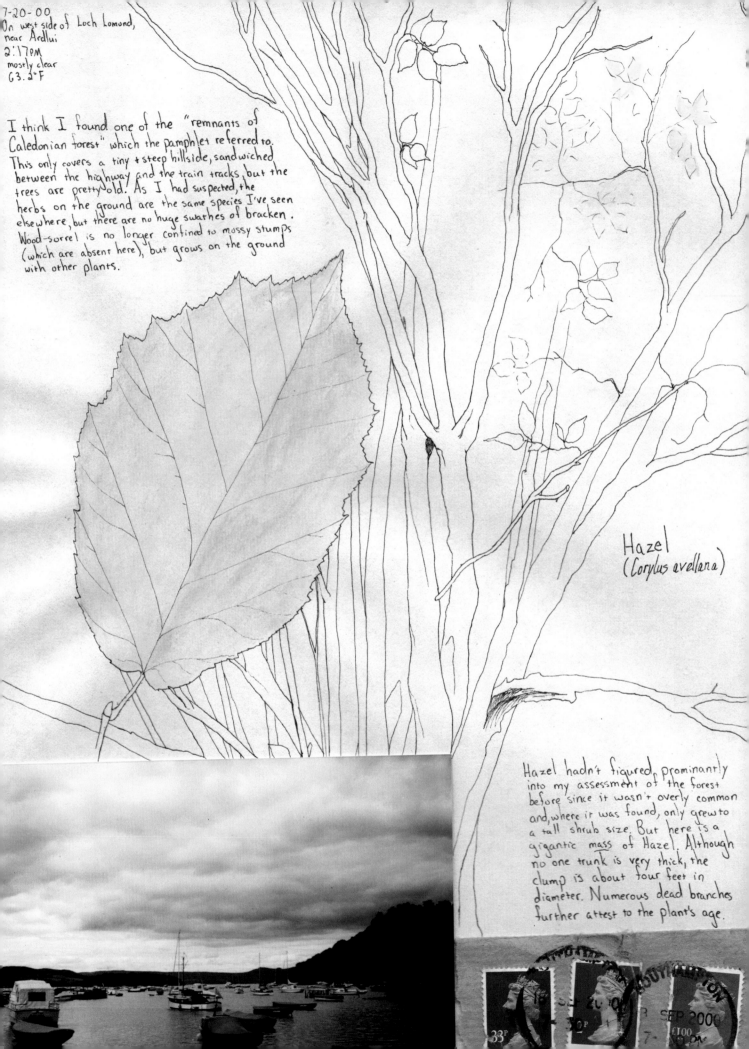

7-20-00
On west side of Loch Lomond,
near Ardlui
2:17PM
mostly clear
63.2°F

I think I found one of the "remnants of
Caledonian forest" which the pamphlet referred to.
This only covers a tiny + steep hillside, sandwiched
between the highway and the train tracks, but the
trees are pretty old. As I had suspected, the
herbs on the ground are the same species I've seen
elsewhere, but there are no huge swathes of bracken.
Wood-sorrel is no longer confined to mossy stumps
(which are absent here), but grows on the ground
with other plants.

Hazel
(Corylus avellana)

Hazel hadn't figured prominantly
into my assessment of the forest
before since it wasn't overly common
and, where it was found, only grew to
a tall shrub size. But here is a
gigantic mass of Hazel. Although
no one trunk is very thick, the
clump is about four feet in
diameter. Numerous dead branches
further attest to the plant's age.

one of those epic ones I love so much in fantasy books. Only here my questing goal is not clear. But then, they never are really. After all, the reason I read the books is because the quest is really an inner one - they have to decide (I'm not quite sure what.) And I always cry at the end, because they've been changed; the most irrevocable endings to quests are the personal changes.

Somehow, I've been assuming the rest of the world has been put on hold while I'm out here, and that's the other painful part. The quester changes, and so do those she holds near & dear & leaves behind & tries to return to. Will we recognize each other in a year? Of course, in fantasy quests, our hero doesn't call home regularly

seal on rocks

There seem to be two dominant species - this one with relatively thin stalks, and the one to the far right with flat, curly wings on the stalk.

Egg or Knotted Wrack
(*Ascophyllum nodosum*)

Dorothy Guidil

Fior

Rùm, shore near Kinloch
2:07 PM
overcast, occassionally sprinkling,
Very midgey
64.2°F

Xanthoria parietina

An enlargement
of the yellow lichen
(c. 4x) shows that
it is made up of
variously shaped,
overlapping scales
with an occassional
fruiting cup.

Bladder Wrack,
(Fucus vesiculosus)

Both species are colored
similarly. The oldest parts are
dark brown, which becomes
more olive-brown in the younger
sections. The bladders and the
youngest tips are golden olive
green.

Thrift
(Armeria m

Thrift grows high enough on the rocks
that it is probably soaked with sea water
seldom, but still more than any other plant
can apparently bear. It forms cushions of
leaves in rocky crevices. Grass-like tufts of
green leaves grow on top of interwoven
brown leaves.

Rùm from afar

Kilmory

Rùm

Kinloch

→ mainland

Lochan
Dornabac

Two ravens flew by as I sat and drew. They were at nearly the same elevation as I was, and I could hear their wings pushing through the air. One gave a questioning croak as it flew past.

7-28-00
Rúm
halfway up Fionchra
1 PM
partly cloudy, with the sun ocassionally shining through;
light wind
71.6°F (in sun)

I found this one little plant nestled down into the grass on the steep mountainside. It's steep enough and high enough that the Bell Heather grows as a groundcover rather than as a low shrub.

← 1.5x

Common Cow-wheat
(Melampyrum pratense)

Burnet Rose
(Rosa pimpinellifolia)

← 1.5x

I sought out this limestone ridge hoping to find lime-loving plants, but I didn't see much out of the ordinary except for a little fern stuck in a cleft in the rocks. On the other hand, there were several areas which had been grazed nearly to the ground, like the machair at Kilmory. Since studies here have shown that the deer prefer grazing in herb-rich areas, there probably were exciting things on this ridge, but the deer got

Exposed rocks on a hillside on Rum, 7-24-00.

7-28-00
Rúm, at the top of Fior
4:10PM
sunny, some clouds
midges!
70.8°F (in shade)

Climbing mountains on Rúm means always seeing stag antlers peeping over the top of the next hill. The stag, of course, is always looki directly toward me, having heard me coming a mile away. But on the last little table on the _____ before I reached th summit, I found a patch of _____ and dawdled there eating until my fingertips _____ ped the last rise and sum _____

Awoke from a dream about a kitten meowing to find loons — "divers" calling in the loch beside my tent...

I was surprised when I reached the top of the mountain and found that it was boggy. I came up here in search of mountain plants, and all I could see was Woodrushes and Bog-cotton and grass. Luckily I had been advised to look for plants on the north-facing rock outcrops, and there I found some fascinating plants, including this Sedum.

Roseroot
(Sedum rosea)

I'm working my way up the mountain, although who knows if I'll ever get there. At lunchtime, I found a marvelous clear pool in a mountain stream & stopped to bathe (no showers at the campsite) & wash my clothes. Sitting on the rocks wearing nothing but my underwear, I heard someone coming. Hastily donning my fleece & throwing a jacket over my legs, I hope I looked like I was wearing clothes. I'm sure wet hair & drying clothes on the rocks nearby gave me away, but he didn't seem to notice, perhaps pretended not to, & chatted before going on up the hill. It's so good to be clean!

Some Charismatic Megafauna of Rúm
Others, less tame and thus not drawn, include Red Deer,
Sea Otters, Seals and, if birds count, Red-throated
Divers (= Loons).)

7-29-00
Guirdil, by bothy (Rùm)
7:30PM
Partly cloudy, sun behind hi
71.2°F

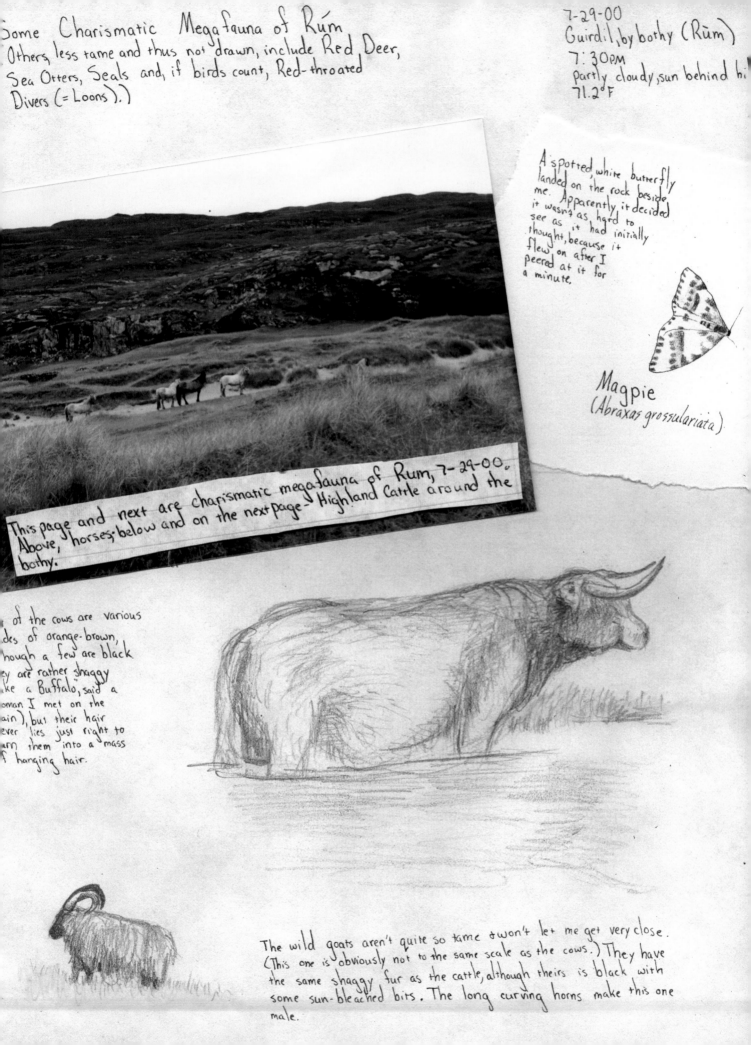

A spotted, white butterfly
landed on the rock beside
me. Apparently it decided
it wasn't as hard to
see as it had initially
thought, because it
flew on after I
peered at it for
a minute.

Magpie
(Abraxas grossulariata)

This page and next are charismatic megafauna of Rum, 7-29-00.
Above, horses; below and on the next page - Highland Cattle around the
bothy.

...of the cows are various
...des of orange-brown,
...hough a few are black
...ey are rather shaggy
...ke a Buffalo," said a
...oman I met on the
...ain), but their hair
...ever lies just right to
...rn them into a mass
...f hanging hair.

The wild goats aren't quite so tame & won't let me get very close.
(This one is obviously not to the same scale as the cows.) They have
the same shaggy fur as the cattle, although theirs is black with
some sun-bleached bits. The long curving horns make this one
male.

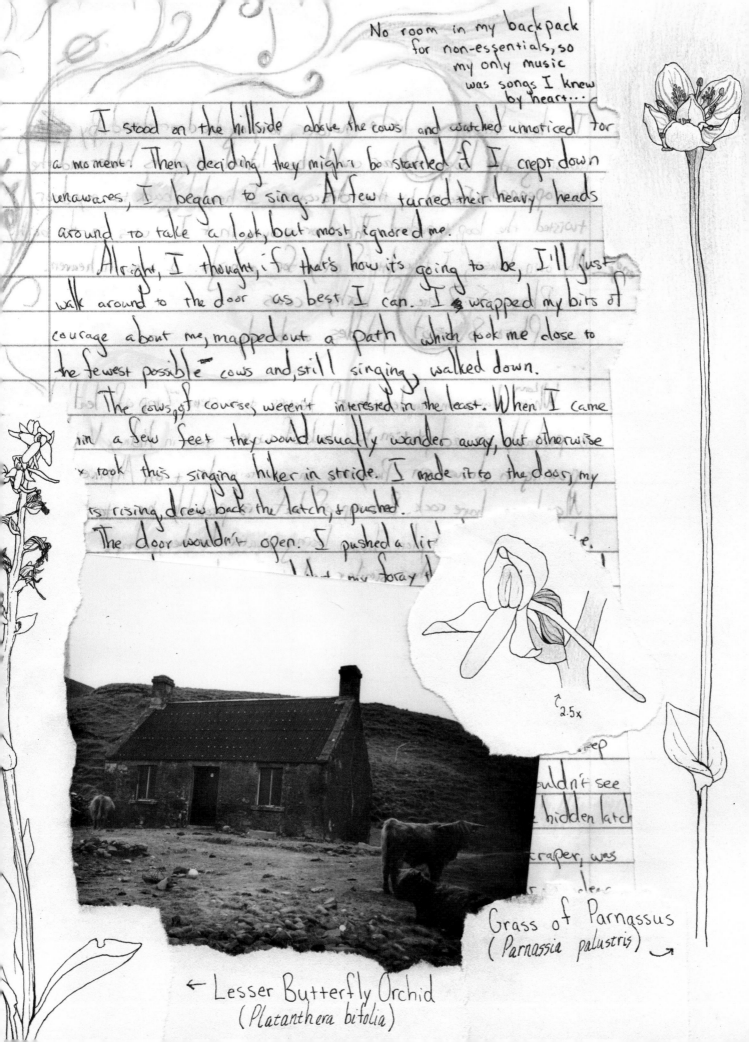

No room in my backpack
for non-essentials, so
my only music
was songs I knew
by heart...

I stood on the hillside above the cows and watched unnoticed for a moment. Then, deciding they might be startled if I crept down unawares, I began to sing. A few turned their heavy heads around to take a look, but most ignored me.

Alright, I thought, if that's how it's going to be, I'll just walk around to the door as best I can. I wrapped my bits of courage about me, mapped out a path which took me close to the fewest possible cows and, still singing, walked down.

The cows, of course, weren't interested in the least. When I came in a few feet they would usually wander away, but otherwise took this singing hiker in stride. I made it to the door, my spirits rising, drew back the latch, & pushed.

The door wouldn't open. I pushed a lit

...d my foray t

...ep

...ouldn't see

...e hidden latch

...craper, was

...clear

Lesser Butterfly Orchid
(Platanthera bifolia)

Grass of Parnassus
(Parnassia palustris) →

↑2.5x

8-3-00
Flander's Moss (peat bog)
near Glasgow
1 PM
partly cloudy, sunny
(then raining)
c. 75°F

Sundews in their natural habitat, and here they are,
... in as a bonus! They're all growing in the
... f the trail. The last few Sundew flowers are
... flowers that hold my interest, in this ...

← Bog Rosemary (Andromeda polifolia)

← 1.5 x

← 3x

← 4x

Common Sundew →
(Drosera rotundifolia)

← 3x

I poked at one of the leaves for a while,
hoping to trick it into closing so that I could
watch. The plant must have rather specific
sensors, because it wasn't fooled by my twig.
However, I found another leaf nearby which
had closed around a fly. In both the front
(to right) and side (to left) views, the fly
can only be seen as a black lump, with an
ocassional leg and wing. The lovely red
hairs have curled inward to form a trap
around the fly, which the leaf is now busy
digesting.

...ne bog is lovely — it's supposed to be a quite undisturbed one. Silver
...irch seemed to be invading (+ being cut out.) I saw an adder,
...ritain's poisonous snake! My first British snake! A salamander
...ashed over a hummock + out of sight. The cranberries were bland
...ut good. I'll bet Amer...
...ran be...
...netha...
...scatio...

1.5x →

Common Butterw...
(Pinguicula vulgaris)

Flood th...

...ral d...

a ne...

...ugh midges,
...ah the plants are more numerous, although
I only found 1 fly and 1 ant in

The bog was very red + green.

Cranberry
(Vaccinium oxycoccos)

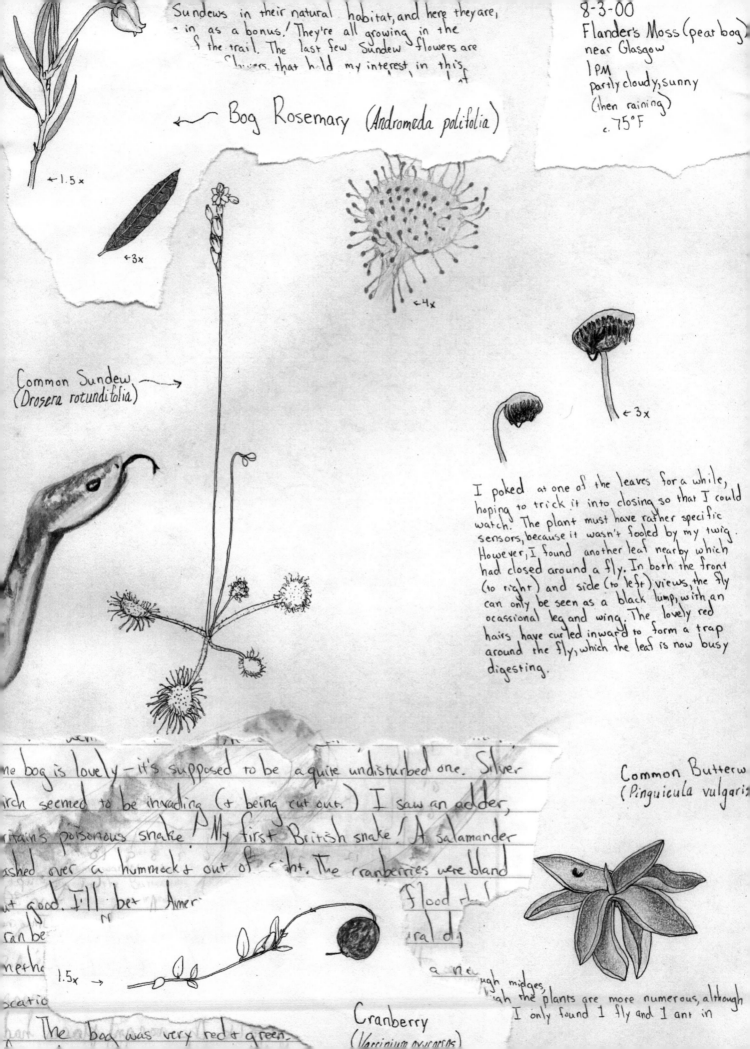

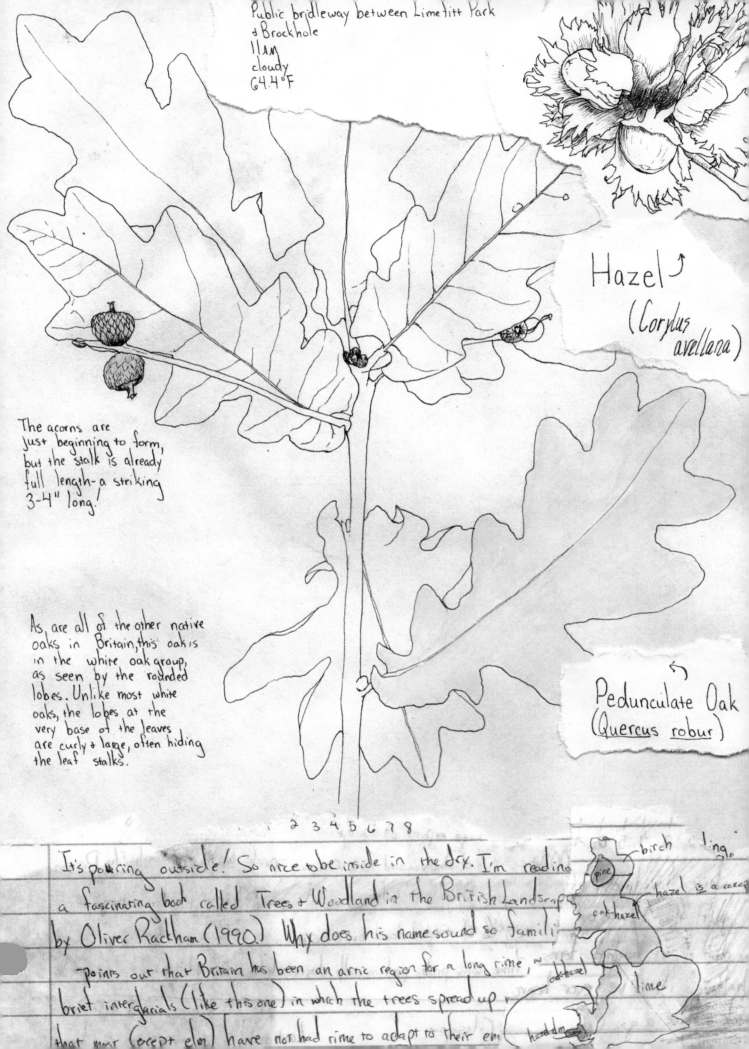

Public bridleway between Limefitt Park
& Brockhole
11 AM
cloudy
64.4°F

Hazel
(Corylus
avellana)

The acorns are
just beginning to form,
but the stalk is already
full length—a striking
3-4" long!

As are all of the other native
oaks in Britain, this oak is
in the white oak group,
as seen by the rounded
lobes. Unlike most white
oaks, the lobes at the
very base of the leaves
are curly & large, often hiding
the leaf stalks.

Pedunculate Oak
(Quercus robur)

1 2 3 4 5 6 7 8

It's pouring outside! So nice to be inside in the dry. I'm reading
a fascinating book called Trees & Woodland in the British Landscape
by Oliver Rackham (1990) Why does his name sound so famili
    points out that Britain has been an arctic region for a long time, w
brief interglacials (like this one) in which the trees spread up a
that most (except elm) have not had time to adapt to their en

birch   ling
pine
hazel is a cara...
oak-hazel
oak-hazel
lime
hazel m

The woods here are more like woods
in Britain, which is probably why I'm wishing I could have seen it
in spring. It's hard to pin down the cause of the naturalness—
continuously forested for hundreds of years, not coppiced for a while
deer fenced out? And who am I to say that it's any mo
than any other forest around? I can really only say
works more like the mature Appalachian forests I know

e seen Red Campions in almost every wood I've
en to in Britain.

8-9-00
Dorothy Farrier's Spr
Wood, near Staveley
11:30AM
overcast & raining
58.4°F

Enchanter's Nightshad
(Circaea lutetiana)

Red Campion
(Silene dioica)

n this wood, they have recently
evived the practice of
oppicing. Trees are cut, leaving
stump, from which sprout
ew little trees. The little
rees are cut every 12-20
ears.

District countryside with sheep
8-10-

nicle
nicula europaea)

Honeysuckle ←

Holly

←Sanicle

Grass

Wood
Sorrel ↗

Fallen
Branch

Herb Robe
(Geranium robertia

day, sitting against a tree, a tiny little rodent ran out of its hole
c. 3 inches from me + into bushes. All I caught was a glimpse of dark
brown sleek fur, I left it 3 rice kernels.

8-12-00
on public bridleway winding
around the south side of
Whitbarrow, near Witherslac[k]
10:20AM
overcast
59.2°F

Hart's-tongue Fern
(*Phyllitis scolopendrium*)
↓

Wall-rue
(*Asplenium ruta-muraria*)

Limestone pavement is, apparently, a perfect habitat [for]
ferns. The pavement is an area of exposed rocks, relative[ly?]
which cracks divide into smaller sections. Some cracks go
down for several feet until the darkness hides the bott[om]
but other cracks, like this one, are much shallower. Ra[in]
and weather have dissolved dips and edges onto the roc[k]

It's strange, that
without the leaflets I co[uld]
Granted, part of it is tha[t the page?]
it looked damaged when [I saw it?]
would have known.

The frond [is all]
rachis, and
is [...]

The fronds are backed by dense white or brown
hairs (white in the youngest fronds.) This makes the leaflets

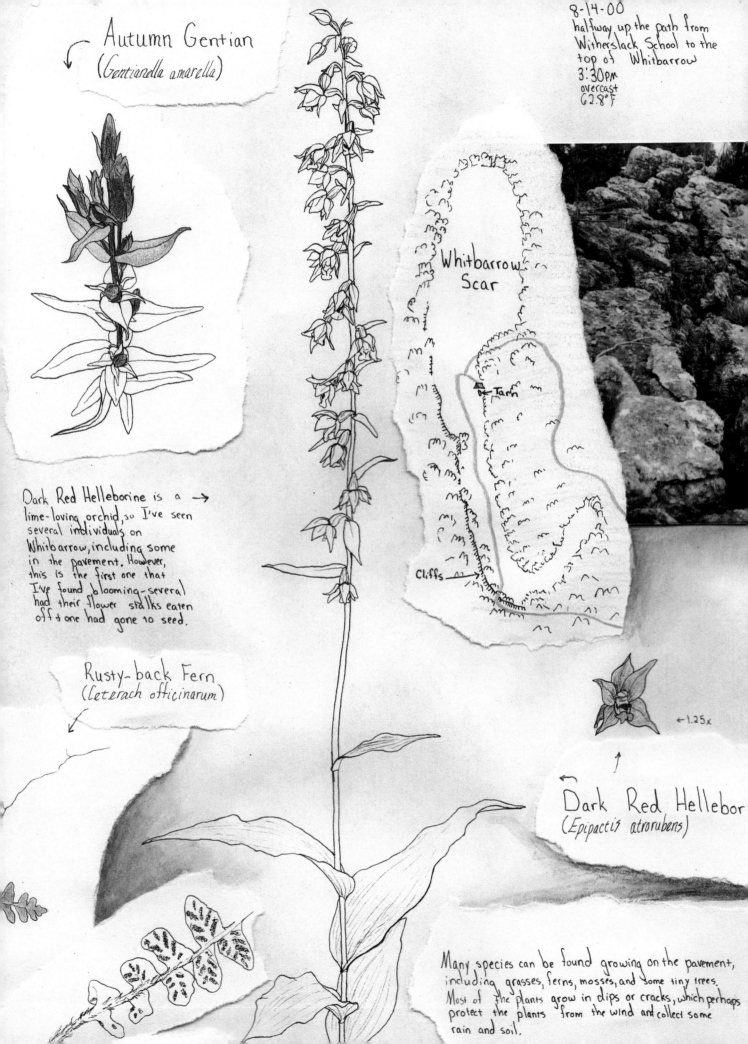

Autumn Gentian
(Gentianella amarella)

8-14-00
halfway up the path from
Witherslack School to the
top of Whitbarrow
3:30 PM
overcast
62.8°F

Whitbarrow
Scar

Tarn

Cliffs

Dark Red Helleborine is a →
lime-loving orchid, so I've seen
several individuals on
Whitbarrow, including some
in the pavement. However,
this is the first one that
I've found blooming-several
had their flower stalks eaten
off + one had gone to seed.

Rusty-back Fern
(Ceterach officinarum)

← 1.25x

Dark Red Hellebor
(Epipactis atrorubens)

Many species can be found growing on the pavement,
including grasses, ferns, mosses, and some tiny trees.
Most of the plants grow in dips or cracks, which perhaps
protect the plants from the wind and collect some
rain and soil.

Above - my tent.
Below - My dear little tarn in the dip below me. It's impossible to see, except from in the dip, on my little ridge, or on the next ridge over. I almost didn't find it & expect no one else will either (without a map.) The deer have paths to it from all directions, but I haven't seen a deer actually at the tarn and nothing has eaten the half-rotten cucumber I left nearby. Whitbarrow - 8-16-00.

Carline Thistle
(*Carlina vulgaris*)

At least half of the limbs on any given yew are leafless & appear dead. The only are found sprouting around the base of trees or growing at the furthest tips of angled away from the wind.

Yew branches don't seem to be able to take the curve of the wind. Instead, the tree the branches on the windward side to die, as well as the upward growing tips so remaining branches are protected from the wind by the main trunk.

I'm going to head back off Whitbarrow today. It's so perfect here that I think I might never have left if not for the ticks which are so numerous that I pick a few dozen off me in the evening & still wake up in the night finding more. My time here has truly flown, but it's time to go— I woke up this morning wanting to look at a map and choose my next home.

Yew
(Taxus baccata)

Berries are getting ripe. The blackberries are mostly black and juicy, the red raspberries are nearly gone, and the berries of several other trees, including Guelder Rose and Whitebeam, are beginning to turn color. I found this fleshy yew fruit on the path, as well as a red Hawthorn fruit.

This bit of limestone pavement is at the top of a little cliff, and the wind apparently blows up & over the cliff, because what trees are here are sharply windswept away from the cliff.

Each tree deals with the wind in its own way. A six-foot holly apparently ignores it; the hazels only grow to about three feet tall; the ashes & birches bend gracefully away from the wind and the yews are windswept angular way.

The path is lined with these sedges when it goes through breaks in the canopy. All of the sedge fruits are ripe and dark brown, nearly black.

I have no idea when Autumn comes to British Isles, and I'm sure it won't truly here for a while, but everywhere I look I see signs that it is coming.

Silver Birch
(Betula pendula)

After several rainy and windy days, the birches have dropped some yellowing leaves. The leaves on the trees are still quite green, but dozens of yellow leaves are sprinkled over the path. The fallen leaves are generally those which have been nibbled on.

8-14-00
Whitbarrow Scar,
by my tent
6:20 PM
some clouds but sunny!
windy
75°F

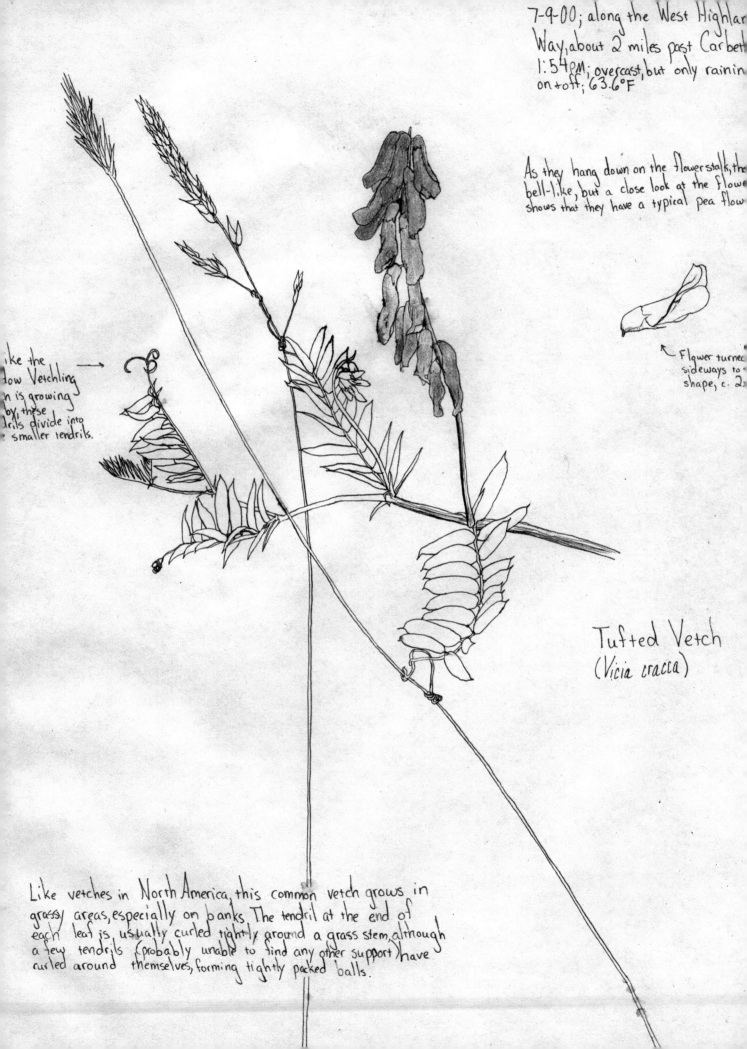

7-9-00; along the West Highla[n]
Way, about 2 miles past Carbet[t]
1:54pm; overcast, but only rainin[g]
on+off; 63.6°F

As they hang down on the flowerstalk, the[y]
bell-like, but a close look at the flowe[r]
shows that they have a typical pea flow[er]

↖ Flower turne[d]
sideways to [see]
shape, c. 2[x]

[l]ike the
[Mead]ow Vetchling
[it] is growing
[near]by, these
[ten]drils divide into
[smaller] smaller tendrils.

Tufted Vetch
(*Vicia cracca*)

Like vetches in North America, this common vetch grows in
grassy areas, especially on banks. The tendril at the end of
each leaf is usually curled tightly around a grass stem, although
a few tendrils (probably unable to find any other support) have
curled around themselves, forming tightly packed balls.

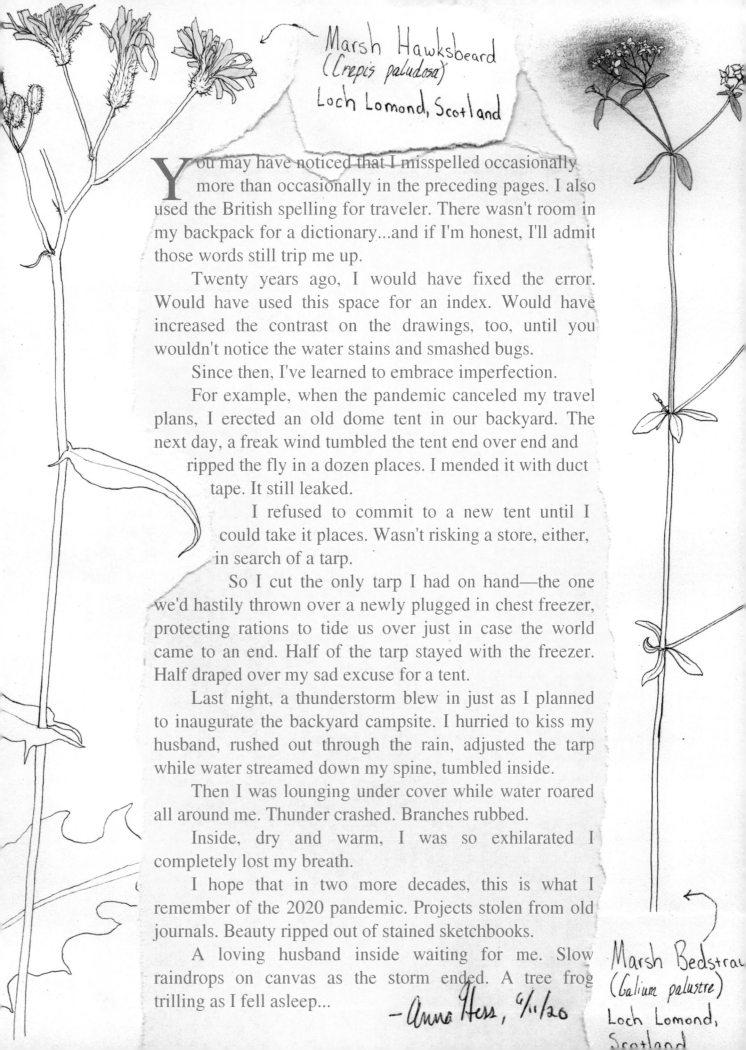

Marsh Hawksbeard
(*Crepis paludosa*)
Loch Lomond, Scotland

Y̲ou may have noticed that I misspelled occasionally
    more than occasionally in the preceding pages. I also
used the British spelling for traveler. There wasn't room in
my backpack for a dictionary...and if I'm honest, I'll admit
those words still trip me up.

Twenty years ago, I would have fixed the error.
Would have used this space for an index. Would have
increased the contrast on the drawings, too, until you
wouldn't notice the water stains and smashed bugs.

Since then, I've learned to embrace imperfection.

For example, when the pandemic canceled my travel
plans, I erected an old dome tent in our backyard. The
next day, a freak wind tumbled the tent end over end and
ripped the fly in a dozen places. I mended it with duct
tape. It still leaked.

I refused to commit to a new tent until I
could take it places. Wasn't risking a store, either,
in search of a tarp.

So I cut the only tarp I had on hand—the one
we'd hastily thrown over a newly plugged in chest freezer,
protecting rations to tide us over just in case the world
came to an end. Half of the tarp stayed with the freezer.
Half draped over my sad excuse for a tent.

Last night, a thunderstorm blew in just as I planned
to inaugurate the backyard campsite. I hurried to kiss my
husband, rushed out through the rain, adjusted the tarp
while water streamed down my spine, tumbled inside.

Then I was lounging under cover while water roared
all around me. Thunder crashed. Branches rubbed.

Inside, dry and warm, I was so exhilarated I
completely lost my breath.

I hope that in two more decades, this is what I
remember of the 2020 pandemic. Projects stolen from old
journals. Beauty ripped out of stained sketchbooks.

A loving husband inside waiting for me. Slow
raindrops on canvas as the storm ended. A tree frog
trilling as I fell asleep...

— Anna Hess, 6/11/20

Marsh Bedstraw
(*Galium palustre*)
Loch Lomond,
Scotland

Last
Night's
Temp.
(in the
inn)
°F
(window
open)

68	
66	
64	
62	
60	
58	

10 11 12 1 2 3 4 5 6

The inn cost £25, but was right where I needed it, and furthermore came with supper & breakfast! Since my original B&B plan had included supper in a restaurant, I actual" came off cheaper than I had planned!

Breakfast was a "whole English breakfast", except that I asked them not to include the bacon (since they don't like it crisp here) & the mushrooms. Which means that I had cereal with milk, then two pieces of toast, cut into triangles & served in a silver rack, two fried eggs, a small tomato, cut in half & fried, a tremendous piece of sausage, orange juice, and of course butter & jam. I ate all of it, except for 3/4 of the sausage, pocketed an extra cereal, & left feeling nearly too stuffed to walk.

The room had also held a hot pot & 4 containers of hot chocolate powder. I had a cup of cocoa last night, a cup this morning, & took the other two along. So I feel very much as if the inn was worth every penny (or pence, rather.)

I met an older couple at breakfast who kindly conversed with me, doing away with the eating alone sensation. They had just met an Ame... me, who came from near the Great Smoky Mountains! It...

A Good, Quick Camp recipe

1. Fill cup to 12 mark w/ water
2. Bring to boil.
3. Fill with pasta to water level.
4. Cook pasta until ready.
5. Don't pour off water.
6. Add 1 package of Cup of Soup Golden Vegetabl...
7. Squeeze mound of twice concentrated tomato on top.
8. Cut in cubes of mild cheddar cheese.
9. Stir & eat.

My new stove let me cook hot meals.

In Glasgow, I hope against hope that I can check my email & maybe even find some folk dancing. I also hope I can get my troublesome tooth looked at.